Things Every Girl Should Know About Her Body

A Girl's Guide to Periods, Growing Up and Loving Your Body

Richa Paliya-Rehan

Things Every Girl Should Know About Her Body

A Girl's Guide to Periods, Growing Up, and Loving Your Body

Richa Paliya-Rehan

❄ LUCKY BOOK PUBLISHING

Paperback ISBN: 978-1-998287-17-8

E-book ISBN: 978-1-998287-18-5

1st edition, August 2024.

"One day you will have the power to make a difference – so use it well."

~ **Mindy Kaling**

My Gift To You

I am so glad you're here!

As my Gift to you, get FREE Access to the
Audiobook of
Things Every Girl Should Know About Her Body
and other Free Resources by scanning the QR Code
below or visiting
www.RichaRehan.com

Praise for Things Every Girl Should Know about Her Body - A Girl's Guide to Periods, Growing Up, and Loving Your Body

"Every young woman should read this book to better understand our amazing female body! This book sheds light on things every girl should know about their body. Every young woman should read this to help better understand how everything works down there and gain confidence about our miraculous lady parts, without the shame!"

- **Jessica Chiarello, Personal Trainer and Prenatal/Postpartum Fitness Expert**

"Richa provides a wealth of knowledge, insights and humour in her debut book. This is a great read for parents and young looking to learn more about their changing bodies. I highly recommend this book."

- **Lesleigh Abbott MD, MD Pediatric Hematology/Oncology**

"Bravo to the author for combining her professional knowledge as a physiotherapist and her advocacy for women's pelvic health to address a complex and often taboo topic . Richa has written her book in an easy-to-understand and creative style that sticks with relevant, bite-sized information about the why, what and how of periods, bridging an information gap and empowering young girls about their bodies. It is an excellent resource for preteens, teens, parents, and educators."

– **Elizabeth Hesp, Leadership Coach and Cultural Intelligence Consultant**

"Where was this book when Aunt Flo showed up unexpectedly, my body started changing and I had no one to explain all these "weird" things that were happening to me!?!?! This book is gold!!! It opens up an honest dialogue about the female body and all its amazing "parts". It's simplistic but informative and helps normalize body talk without shame or embarrassment. Richa's "matter-of-fact" tone about the female body is done with humour, sensitivity, simplicity and professionalism. A must-read for everyone, not just girls. Hopefully, there will be one for boys and their bodies in the future."

– **Fran Garton, Pain Reduction Coach, Body-Positive Personal Trainer**

"Richa brings much needed education and awareness for teens and tweens in a very light hearted language. When a girl hits puberty there are so many questions and fears buzzing in her brain. Why am I feeling the way I am feeling? What will happen next? Am I the only one going through this? With changing times girls are provided with more education and support but still the notion of "Girls have to deal with this, it is normal" is still around. They are shy to ask Questions. This book gives an insight into many of those unanswered questions. Richa is passionate and dedicated towards women's wellness especially around pelvic health and this book is an empowerment to start early. This book is a must read for every girl and their Mom's for a happier and healthier transition."

– **Dr. Ruchi Shah, Doctor of Physical Therapy, Pelvic Floor Therapist and Postpartum Specialist**

"A brilliant handbook for parents and young women alike, daring to address the once-taboo topics of female bodies and puberty head-on. This book fills a crucial void for those navigating this pivotal stage of life without guidance. It seamlessly blends technical terminology with familiar, everyday language, ensuring accessibility across various age groups.

It's high time we shattered the silence surrounding so many needlessly taboo subjects. By offering a clear vocabulary and normalizing what should be commonplace, it empowers readers to embrace these conversations with confidence and clarity."

> – **Rosy, the Mortgageless Mentor, Author, Don't Have Sex Nine Months Before Christmas and other Practical Financial Tips**

"Every young woman should read this book to better understand our amazing female body! This book sheds light on the amazing female body. Every young woman should read this to help better understand how everything works down there and gain confidence about our miraculous lady parts, without the shame! This book is so easy to read and I love the way she describes this as the "body map".

> – **Fahamia Koudra, Physician**

"This book is a godsend for teen and tween girls curious about their bodies. It uses a perfect blend of humour and seriousness, explaining everything in a way they can understand. It uses "proper language" alongside relatable teen lingo, tackling even the most awkward topics girls might be too shy to ask about. "Things Every Girl Should Know About Their Body" aims to empower girls and banish any feelings of shame about the natural changes their bodies are going through. It provides essential information in a relatable way, promoting body positivity and self-acceptance."

- **Mel Hagn, Personal Trainer and Nutrition Coach, Online Body Transformation Coach for Women**

"This marvelous book is a celebration of girls and women, and our amazing bodies. It is a motivating and uplifting read – a real feminine gem, a pearl of wisdom. Richa lovingly and respectfully shares about all the fascinating changes that occur in a girl's body during puberty. She makes the terms and complex physiological content comprehensible for the reader, and the book becomes an empowerment journey where girls become their own super heroes and explorers of their anatomy and the changing landscape. What a gift! A must read for the girls in all our lives."

- **Shelley A. Murdock, Fitness Instructor, Personal Trainer, Yoga Teacher, Author of HEALTHY & FIT FOR LIFE - THE STARTER KIT FOR WOMEN OVER 50**

"With warmth and clarity, Richa provides valuable support and guidance, making this book a must-read for any girl seeking understanding and confidence during this transformative time."

- **Manali Haridas, Spiritual Wellness Coach, Zen for You & Author of " You Got This Mom" Handbook**

"This book provides comprehensive, accessible information on the female body, demystifying many topics that are often overlooked or misunderstood. With clear explanations and practical advice, it empowers women to take charge of their health and well-being. Whether you're a young girl just starting to learn about your body or an adult looking to deepen your understanding, this book is a valuable resource. I highly recommend it to anyone seeking to enhance their knowledge and confidence about their body."

- **Sarah Boyd, Personal Trainer and Health Coach**

Contents

ACKNOWLEDGEMENTS

This book is dedicated to every young girl who courageously embraces and cherishes her body, celebrating its uniqueness without the burden of comparison. Your strength and self-love inspire us all to appreciate the beauty within ourselves and others.

I am deeply grateful to my wonderful husband, Gaurav Rehan, for breaking societal norms with his equal participation in household chores and for continuously reminding me of my unstoppable potential.

To my daughter, Meera Rehan, and my niece, Sia Nagar, you are my guiding light and inspiration to challenge taboos and stigma, creating a better world for the women of the next generation. You are an ongoing reminder for me to be the best version of myself that I can be.

In loving memory of my father, Govind Paliya, whose belief in the power of information and writing continues to inspire me. Your legacy lives on in every word written.

To my mother, Rekha Paliya, thank you for instilling in me the importance of financial and emotional independence, and for being a constant source of strength.

To my sisters, Shilpa and Pragati, you have always been my unwavering support, being there with me through life's challenges with love and encouragement.

A heartfelt thanks to the rest of my big family and friends for always cheering for me, believing in my dreams, and standing by my side through it all. Thanks for supporting me and loving me through all the crazy. I've been able to step into the fullness of who I am because of it. I am so lucky to be so loved.

I, also extend my deepest gratitude to my profession, as I would have never been passionate about this journey if I were not a pelvic physiotherapist. Thank you to all my patients for sharing their stories and inspiring me to write this book.

To my publishing team, Samantha & Simar! Your unwavering support and guidance have been the cornerstone of this endeavor. Without you, I would have never believed in my ability to write and bring this book to fruition. You've inspired me to embrace my role as an author, and for that, I am eternally grateful. Thank you for being the exact team my heart had hoped for. Your belief in me has been a privilege and a blessing.

You have all helped me realize this vision and I am so, so grateful.

~ Richa xo

PREFACE

Dear Readers,

This is not another period education or sex education book.

The genesis of this book sprouted in my mind when I had my daughter Meera, and I felt an urgent desire to foster a generation unapologetically empowered, free from the shackles of shame or secrecy surrounding their bodies.

I dream of raising a generation unafraid to talk openly about their bodies, periods, and more. This book is a celebration of our bodies – incredible vessels deserving of understanding, respect, and appreciation.

Together, let's embrace the power of knowledge, shatter the barriers of taboo, and pave the way for a generation unafraid to embrace every aspect of their bodily journey. My goal is simple: to equip you with the knowledge, tools, and confidence to understand and appreciate your body.

In today's world, discussions about female anatomy, hygiene, and period health are often shrouded in secrecy, shame, and misinformation. As a result, many girls grow up feeling confused, embarrassed, or even ashamed of their bodies. But they don't have to.

As you embark on this journey of self-discovery and empowerment, remember that you are not alone. I am here as your guide, your ally, and your advocate. I hope that this book serves as a beacon of light, illuminating the path toward a lifetime of health, happiness, and self-love.

With love and solidarity,

~ Richa xo

INTRODUCTION

Things Every Girl Should Know About Her Body

Dear Amazing Teens and Tweens,

Hey there! I hope this letter finds you smiling. I'm super excited to share something special with you—the book "Things Every Girl Should Know About Her Body." Yep, that's the title, and it's all about YOU!

Are you feeling lost in the sea of confusing info out there? From ads promising brighter armpits and scented vaginal washes for your lady bits to conflicting information over shaving, menstrual products, and genital health, it's like a jungle out there. But fear not—this book's got your back (and your front)! It's like your personal guide to cut through the nonsense and get to the real deal.

Plus, it introduces you to those body parts that

are usually kept under wraps. You know, the ones that never make it to dinner table conversations? But guess what? Without them, we wouldn't even be here! Yep, I'm serious! So let's dive in and get to know ourselves a little better, shall we?

As you're growing up, your body is changing in amazing ways, both inside and outside. But sometimes, there are parts of your body that seem like a mystery. This book is your guide to solving those mysteries and understanding how things work "down there."

Why Should You Learn About Your Body?

When you know how your body works, you feel stronger, and more confident, and you learn to love yourself just the way you are. Sometimes, people say stuff that makes us feel a bit awkward about our bodies. But you know what? It's okay to talk about it and ask questions. This book is like your friend who will teach you all about your body parts that no one wants to talk about.

I wrote this book because I want you to feel like a total boss. No more feeling confused or unsure. You deserve to have all the cool info about your body!

So let's jump into these pages together and let the adventure begin! You're gonna be the coolest kid in class knowing all about your body. Got questions nobody else has answers to? I've got you covered!

Think of this book as a map that's going to show you all the cool places in your body. It's like a super fun adventure that will help you understand your mystery box better. By the time we're done, you'll feel like a body expert ready to take on the world!

Are you excited? Get ready to learn amazing things about your body and how it works, especially the stuff "down there." Let's start this awesome journey together!

CHAPTER 1

My Introduction to Aunt Flo aka Lady in Red aka Periods

This is My Story About My Mystery Box aka My Genitals

Alright, let me paint you a picture: I'm 12, just chilling at my aunt's house, minding my own business when WHAM! My first period hits me like a ton of bricks. And let me tell you, I was NOT ready for it.

Sure, I'd heard some whispers from my girlfriends about periods, but it was all super vague. So when Aunt Flo decided to make her grand entrance, I was totally clueless.

Summoning all the courage I had, I finally spilled the beans to my aunt. And that's when she introduced me to the magical world of sanitary pads. Let's just say it was a real eye-opener.

But here's where it gets really funny (or cringy, depending on your perspective): I was absolutely petrified of tampons! I thought tampons went into the pee hole! Yeah, I know, major facepalm moment. It took me until I was 15 to muster up the courage to give them a shot. Can you blame me? I had this wild idea that they went into the same place as pee comes out, and you can imagine how that messed with my head. So, needless to say, I wasn't exactly jumping at the chance to try them out because I thought I would have to change my tampon and take it out every time I went pee (such a pain if it was true, right?)

And let's not even get started on the whole "how many holes are down there" debacle. Talk about embarrassing!

But despite all the awkwardness and confusion, I eventually figured things out and learned a ton about my body and navigating the wild world of periods. And hey, if sharing my story can help break down some taboos and spark conversations, then it's all worth it!

CHAPTER 2

Meet Padma "The Pelvis"

Get ready to meet someone super awesome in your body world – Padma the Pelvis! Padma is like the captain of your lower body team, and in this chapter, we're going to learn all about this amazing buddy who keeps things running smoothly down there.

The word "pelvis" comes from the Latin word for "basin" or "container," which is fitting because the pelvis is indeed a basin-shaped structure in the human body. It's a sturdy framework made up of bones. Imagine Pelvis as a strong and reliable foundation at the bottom of your body. Your Pelvis is made up of special bones like the hip bones, (pubic bones at the front), the sacrum, and the coccyx, which is the tail bone at the end. These bones work together to give you balance, strength, and flexibility. Just like the base of a cool fort, Pelvis keeps everything in place.

The pelvis plays a crucial role in supporting the spine and protecting the internal organs in the abdominal and pelvic regions. Its shape is what gives it the appearance of a basin or container, and this is why it was named "pelvis" in Latin, a name that has stuck through the ages in anatomical terminology. Umm but I don't like to call it basin, so we will call it "Padma," the lotus-like pelvis, indeed a fitting name that reflects its beauty and importance in your body.

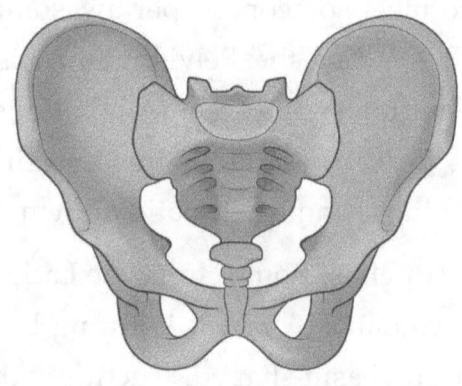

Pelvis, in human anatomy, lotus-shaped complex of bones that connects the trunk and the legs, supports and balances the trunk, and contains and supports the intestines, the urinary bladder, uterus and rectum.

The Hip Connection

Ever tried doing the twist or shaking your hips or twerking like those TikTok trends? That's Pelvis having fun with you! Your hip bones are part of Pelvis, and they're the reason you can do those cool moves.

Whether you're dancing, skipping, or walking, your hips are the helpers that make it all possible.

Guess what? Pelvis is like a superhero protector for important stuff like the bladder, uterus, and rectum. It's like a fortress, keeping these precious organs safe. Pelvis makes sure these important areas are safe and sound, just like a trusty guardian. Think of your pelvis as the solid foundation of a house. It's the strong frame that holds up your spine, legs, and some important organs.

Breathe Easy with Pelvis

Breathing feels awesome, right? Pelvis is best friends with your diaphragm, a super muscle that helps you breathe. So, every time you take a deep breath, Pelvis and your diaphragm are working together to keep you feeling calm and relaxed.

Growing and Changing Together

Just like you're growing and changing, Pelvis grows and changes too. As you become older, Pelvis shifts and adjusts to fit your body perfectly. When you're on the path to becoming a teenager, Pelvis gets ready for some special changes that come with growing up. For some people, especially women, the pelvis becomes a superhero during childbirth. It helps guide the baby out safely.

Pelvis is also your Posture Pal

The pelvis doesn't just protect; it supports too. It gives your spine a strong base and houses muscles that help you stand tall. Think of it as your body's secret helper, making sure you don't slouch.

Showing Love to Padma aka Pelvis

Padma loves some care and attention, just like a good friend does. By eating healthy, staying active, and sitting up straight, you're showing Padma some love. And if you ever feel anything strange around your pelvis, remember, it's okay to talk to a grown-up you trust about it.

And that's Pelvis, your fantastic friend! Pelvis helps you move, keeps important parts safe, and even plays a part in your breathing. So, embrace your pelvis, have fun with your moves!

I think of the pelvis like a lotus, providing a home to some of the most important parts of our body.

Fun Pelvis Facts

- Your pelvis is unique, like your fingerprint. No one else has the same pelvis as you.

- When you dance, your pelvis is the star. Those hip movements on the dance floor? You can thank your pelvis for that!

- Archaeologists study ancient pelvis bones to learn about people who lived a long time ago. It's like a history book written in bones.

So, there you have it—the pelvis, your body's strong supporter and protector. It keeps you moving, dancing, and living your life to the fullest!

CHAPTER 3

The V-Venture: "The Vulva" and "The Vagina" aka Confusion

Oh Wait, Vulva and Vagina Are Different?!

Imagine this: you're standing in front of a mirror, trying to figure out the mysteries between your legs, but everything feels like a puzzle. You've got your clitoris, labia majora, labia minora, urethral opening, vaginal opening, perineum, and anus – each with its own unique role. Despite this amazing landscape, there's still so much confusion about what's down there. Let's clear things up and learn some key terms first.

Vagina, Vulva, Labia, and Clitoris: Breaking It Down

Ever mixed up the words vulva and vagina?

You're not alone! These terms can feel like trying to crack a secret code. It's like thinking puzzle pieces fit together when they actually belong to different sets. We're going to sort out these words for you, just like organizing your colorful building blocks.

Do you have questions like, "Wait, aren't vulva and vagina the same thing?"

"How many holes are there?" "Labia? What's that?" "Is the clitoris just like a mini-penis?" These are common thoughts, and if you've had them, don't worry – you're not alone. Let's dive into these questions together.

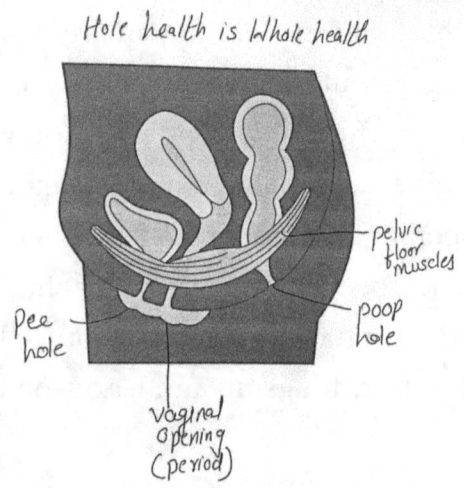

There is a total of 3 holes in the genital area. There are two holes in the vulva: the opening to the vagina (For period blood) and the opening to the urethra (pee hole). The third hole is the anus (poop hole AKA butthole).

How Many Holes Do Vulva Owners Have?

Urethral Opening (Pee hole): This small opening allows urine to exit your body.

Vaginal Opening (Period blood hole): This is where menstrual blood exits during periods and the space through which babies are born. It's also the pathway for sexual intercourse, allowing for physical closeness and creating new life.

Anus (Poop hole): This is where waste is eliminated from the body.

What's the Vulva, Anyway?

First things first, let's get our vocab straight. The vulva is the external part of the female genitalia. It's often confused with the vagina, but they're different parts. The vulva includes everything you can see on the outside, while the vagina is the internal tube leading to the uterus. Here's a quick breakdown of the vulva parts:

- Labia Majora: These are the "outer lips" that protect the more delicate parts inside. They can be different sizes and colors, and that's totally normal.

- Labia Minora: These are the "inner lips," located inside the labia majora. They can be short or long and often stick out past the outer lips.

- Clitoris: This small but mighty part is super sensitive and can bring a lot of pleasure. It's located at the top where the labia minora meet.
- Urethral Opening: This tiny hole is where pee comes out, just below the clitoris.
- Vaginal Opening: This is the entrance to the vagina, where menstrual blood exits, and where tampons go in.

The word "vulva" comes from Latin, meaning "wrapper" or "covering." Knowing the proper term helps us talk about it accurately and with respect. Imagine if your name is Sarah, and people keep calling you Shelley!

The Vulva's Jobs

- Protection: The labia protect the sensitive internal parts.
- Pleasure: The clitoris is packed with nerve endings and is all about feeling good.
- Passage: The vaginal opening is key for menstrual blood to leave the body and for intercourse.

Anatomy Lesson: Vagina, the Superhero Tunnel

The word "vagina" means "sheath" or "scabbard"

– like a cover for a sword. People have called it different things for ages, like "vajayjay," "hoo-ha," or just "down there." In science class, it's the vagina. Knowing the proper name helps us talk about it with confidence and respect.

The vagina is like the magical bridge linking your vulva to your uterus. This dynamic passageway plays a starring role, from allowing menstrual blood to exit to being a pathway for menstrual cups and tampons.

Busting Myths

Myth: All vulvas look the same.

Fact: Vulvas come in all shapes, sizes, and colors. Each one is unique!

Myth: The vulva should smell like flowers.

Fact: The vulva has a natural scent. A strong or unusual odor can be a sign to see a doctor.

Final Thoughts

The vulva is an amazing part of the body that deserves to be understood and respected. Learning about it helps you take better care of yourself and feel more confident. Don't be afraid to ask questions and learn more. Knowledge is power, and you've got this!

So Hi Again, "The Vulva"

Just like each person's face or fingerprints are one-of-a-kind, so are vulvas! They come in many shapes and colors, just like flowers in a garden. Every vulva is different, and that's totally okay. Your vulva is like your body's special mark – it's unique and belongs only to you.

Embracing Different Shapes and Sizes

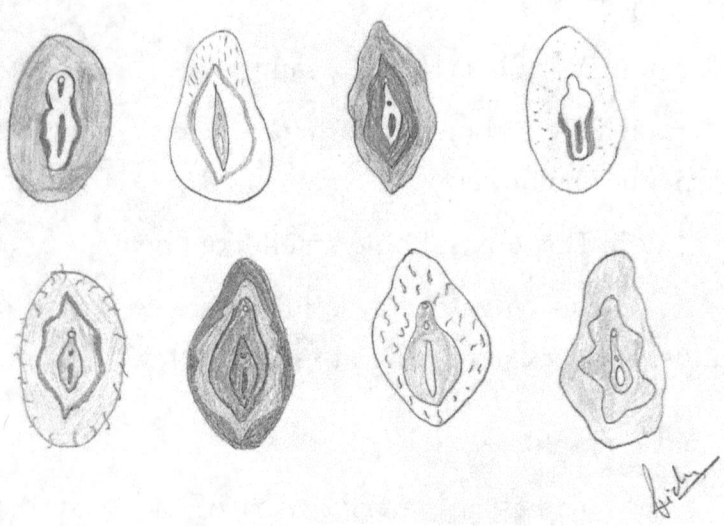

There's no such thing as a "normal" looking vulva. Just like faces, every vulva and vagina is unique — they all have the same parts, but each one looks a little different, and

Think about how people have different heights and body shapes. Well, vulvas are the same! Some may look small, while others might seem bigger and more noticeable. Some vulvas have longer parts, and others have rounder parts. All these differences are completely normal and wonderful.

Instead of comparing yourself to others, it's better to appreciate the amazing variety of vulvas. Imagine if we all celebrated all the colors and shapes of vulvas.

Colors That Make Each Vulva Special

Just like how flowers can be red, yellow, or purple, vulvas come in various colors too. They might be light pink, lighter brown, darker brown, black, or anything in between. These differences in color are like a badge of honor that shows how unique we all are.

No More Feeling Ashamed

In the past, people didn't talk much about vulvas and felt embarrassed about them. But things are changing now. We're learning that there's nothing to be ashamed of. It's okay to talk about vulvas and understand them better. By learning and talking, we can stop feeling embarrassed and start feeling proud of our bodies.

Your Own Amazing Story

Your vulva is a part of your body that's just as special as your favorite toy or book. It's been with you through many parts of your life. Just like how you grow and change, your vulva does too. It might look different as you get older or if you become a parent. All these changes are normal and part of life.

When you look at yourself in the mirror, remember that your vulva tells the story of your life. It's like a map of all the things you've experienced. Every mark, spot, and wrinkle has a story to tell, and that's something to be proud of.

In a world where people sometimes want everyone to be the same, celebrating the different types of vulvas is important. By loving your own vulva, you're saying that being different is a wonderful thing. And when we all celebrate our differences, the world becomes a better place for everyone.

How to Take Care of Your Vulva

The Natural Harmony: Caring for Your Self-Cleaning Vulva Just like how a delicate ecosystem thrives within a rainforest, your vulva maintains its own natural balance. It's a remarkable self-cleaning system that requires minimal intervention. Let's explore how to keep your vulva happy and healthy without disrupting its innate harmony.

- Warm Water: During your daily shower, cleanse your vulva gently with warm water. Avoid using harsh soaps or scented products as they can disrupt the natural pH balance and cause irritation.

- Front to Back: When wiping after using the toilet, always remember to wipe from front to back. This helps prevent any unwanted bacteria from moving towards the sensitive vaginal area.

- Breathable Underwear: Choose cotton underwear that allows air to circulate. This helps keep your vulva dry and prevents excess moisture that could lead to discomfort.

- Loose Clothing: Opt for loose-fitting clothes that don't trap heat and moisture. This is particularly important in hot and humid weather.

- Skip Douching: Douching disrupts the natural balance of your vulva and can even lead to infections. Trust your body's ability to maintain its cleanliness.

- Limit Scented Products: Avoid using scented pads, tampons, or sprays. These can cause irritation and mess with your body's natural scent.

Why Knowing the Right Terminologies Matters

Guess what? It's totally okay to wonder about all

this stuff! In fact, it's way more than just knowing names – it's about owning your body, your bits, and your beauty. By knowing what's down there, you're taking a stand against any hush-hush vibes and saying, "Hey, I'm in charge of my body!"

Knowledge is Power and Fun Too!

Remember that knowing about your own body is like holding a superpower – it's a power that's way more amazing than any gadget or trick. Embrace the adventure of understanding your vagina, vulva, labia, and clitoris. It's all about celebrating what makes you, well, uniquely you! So let's lift the veil on the mystery and enjoy every bit of discovering our incredible bodies.

Trusting Your Body

In a world filled with products promising freshness and cleanliness, it's important to remember that your vulva knows how to take care of itself. By adopting gentle and minimalistic hygiene practices, you're allowing your body to thrive naturally.

Embracing the self-cleaning wonder of your vulva isn't just about maintaining physical health; it's a celebration of the incredible resilience and intelligence of your body. Trusting in its abilities and treating it with kindness is a beautiful act of self-care.

Your vulva is super sensitive and needs some extra love and care. Washing it gently with water is usually enough to keep it clean. You don't need to use any fancy soaps or sprays because those can sometimes cause irritation.

Getting Comfortable

Sometimes talking about our genitals can feel a little weird, but it's important to know and understand your own body. If you ever have questions or feel curious, it's totally okay to ask a trusted adult or a doctor. Learning about your body is a journey, and you're the explorer!

Remember, your genitals are just one part of your amazing body. They're unique, wonderful, and they're there to help you grow and thrive. So embrace your body, get to know it better, and always treat it with kindness and respect. You're on an exciting adventure of self-discovery, and your body is your best companion!

CHAPTER 4

Pelvic Floor Muscles – Your Hidden Superheroes

Yo squad! Ready to dive into the secret world of your pelvic floor muscles? These cool girls might be out of sight, but trust me, they're major players in keeping you feeling epic every day. Let's unpack what these muscle heroes–no wait, it's all about heroines in this book–so let's unpack what these muscle heroines are all about!

What's Up with Pelvic Floor Muscles?

Imagine this: a hammock, but it's made of muscles and tissues, swinging from your tailbone (that's at your back) to your pubic bone (right up front). This muscle hammock is what we call your pelvic floor. It's the VIP lounge holding up your bladder (where the pee hangs out), your rectum (team poop's clubhouse), and for the ladies, your uterus. Cool beans, right?

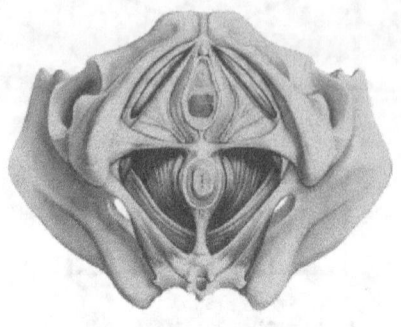

Your pelvic floor consists of muscles and connective tissues that support important organs in your pelvis, like your bladder, bowel (large intestine) and internal reproductive organs. Your pelvic floor muscles hold these organs in place while also providing the flexibility to assist with bodily functions like peeing, pooping and sex.

Why Should You Even Care?

Here's why these muscles deserve some hype:

- Organ Support Squad: Just like a hammock cradles you, your pelvic floor muscles are the support crew for your bladder, uterus, and rectum.

- Pee and Poop Boss: They're like the bouncers at the bathroom door, giving you the power to decide when to go. Healthy pelvic floor muscles = no pee leaks or bedwetting.

- Posture and Stability Pros: They keep you standing tall and steady. Good posture means less back pain and a healthier you!

How Do They Do Their Thing?

Think of blowing up a balloon. Inhaling? It gets bigger. Exhaling? It shrinks. Your pelvic floor muscles work kinda like that, flexing and relaxing without making a scene.

Everyday Superpowers

- Sneeze and Cough Guard: Ever wondered why you don't pee your pants when you sneeze or cough, unlike some of the moms who didn't do pelvic floor physio after giving birth? Hats off to your pelvic floor muscles!

- Jump and Run Shield: These muscles cushion the shock when you jump or sprint, keeping your organs from throwing a wild party inside.

Uh-oh, Muscle Trouble?

Sometimes, these muscle heroines can get a bit lazy (weak) or too tense. Here are some SOS signals:

- Leaky Faucet: Oops! Dribbled a bit while laughing, sneezing, or jogging? Time to tune up those muscles.

- Rush Hour: Always racing to the loo? Yep, another heads-up.

- Bathroom Struggles: Trouble getting started or

feeling like you haven't emptied completely? Check your muscle hammock.

- Pain in the Base: Aching down there, especially in your lower belly or pelvis? Red flag!

- Feeling the Pressure: If it feels like something's pushing down in your pelvis, that's not cool.

- Ouch in the Game: Discomfort during sports or just while sitting around too long? Time to investigate.

Working on Your Pelvic Floor Muscles

Great news: you can totally beef up these muscles with some help from a pelvic health physiotherapist. Like leg day, but for your pelvic floor!

Let's Talk Pelvic Health

Chit-chatting about pelvic health might sound awks, but it's chill once you get the hang of it. Here's how to keep it real:

- Use Cool Comparisons: Like the hammock and balloon we talked about.

- Be Curious: Got questions? Shoot! Ask a trusted adult or doctor.

- Spread the Word: Bet your friends have the same

questions. Sharing is caring, so keep them in the loop.

Conclusion

Your pelvic floor muscles are like undercover superheroes, always on duty to keep you rocking a healthy and strong vibe. By getting to know them and showing them some love, you're doing your body a solid. Keep it up, Girl!

CHAPTER 5

Meet Ms. H, "The Hymen"

Meet the Hymen: Like a Tiny Curtain

Hello friends! In this chapter, we're going to talk about something called the hymen. It's a small, delicate piece near the entrance of the vagina, and it's a bit of a mystery. Let's learn more about what it does and why it's important.

Think of the hymen as a small curtain at the door to the vagina. It's a natural guard there for a reason. While scientists aren't entirely sure what it does, they think it helps protect the inside of the body when we're growing up.

Different Shapes and Sizes

Hymens aren't all the same. They come in various

shapes and sizes. Some look like a half-moon, others like a ring, and some even have a little wall in the middle. It's like a tiny fingerprint—it's unique for each person.

Myth Busting: Hymens and Virginity

Here's an important fact: the hymen doesn't tell us if someone is a virgin or not. Some people think it does, but that's not true. Hymens can change naturally over time because of things like sports, using tampons, or just growing up. Virginity is a personal thing and it's not about the hymen.

Hymens Around the World

Different cultures have their own ideas about hymens. In some places, having an intact hymen was seen as a sign of purity. But remember, times change and we should respect different beliefs and traditions.

Hymen and Pain: Getting Help

Sometimes the hymen can cause pain during activities like sex or using tampons. If that happens, it's essential to talk to a doctor. They can help you and talk to you about it more.

The Hymen: A Small but Interesting Part

The hymen might be tiny, but it's part of a bigger

story—the story of our bodies, their diversity, and how we feel about them. It reminds us that our bodies are unique, and there's no one right way for them to be.

In the end, the hymen is a little mystery in the big story of our bodies. It's time to clear up any misunderstandings and appreciate how amazing our bodies are!

CHAPTER 6

Meet Ms V, the Vagina

Vagina Basics

Hello my curious friends! Next we are going to learn about the vagina. It's a hidden treasure in your body, and we're going to uncover its secrets in a fun and easy way. You can call it Vayjanti Box, Vajayjay, etc., etc., whatever you want as it's your vagina. Now, let's venture inside.

Let's start with the basics. The vagina is a super helper in your body. It does many important jobs:

1. The Love Place: Your vagina is not just any part; it's the special place where love and closeness happen. It's like the entrance to a special event.

2. The Magic Cleaner: Imagine having a magic cleaner in your room. Well, your vagina has a special way to keep itself clean. It makes a special

liquid to stay fresh. So leave it alone and don't try to clean it with all the scented products available in the market.

3. Helping with Babies: When it's time to make a baby, the vagina is like the starting line. Tiny things called sperm race to meet an egg. And when a baby is born, the vagina stretches to let the baby come out.

4. Feeling Good: The vagina can feel lots of good things. It's a place full of tiny feelers that make it feel nice when touched.

5. Different and Unique: Like people, no two vaginas are the same. They can look different and that's perfectly okay.

Questions About Vaginas

- What's That Smell? Vaginas have their own special smell that can change. But if the smell seems strange or too strong, you can talk to a doctor. But it's not supposed to smell like flowers the way it's shown in vagina cleaning products ads, so stay away from those products unless prescribed by your healthcare provider.

- Feeling Comfortable: The vagina can stretch, but if you ever feel uncomfortable, you can try different ways or use something called lubrication to make it feel better.

- Ready for Fun: Lubrication is like a sign that the body is ready for fun. It changes when you're excited.

So there you go—the vagina, a special part of your body. It does important things and can feel really nice. Remember to take care of it because it's a special part of you!

Vagina: The Superhero Tunnel of Your Body

It's like the magical bridge that links your vulva, where it all begins, to your uterus. This dynamic passageway plays a starring role in both life's grand entrances as babies and menstrual blood make their exit in style. But wait, there's more! It's also the go-to spot for some exciting guests: penises, fingers, playful sex toys, and those trusty companions, menstrual cups and tampons. And here's a fun fact: your vagina has a secret superpower—it's super stretchy, expanding like a champ when you're feeling all kinds of turned on. So whether it's for exiting, entering, or exploring, your vagina is here to make life's adventures exciting and, well, quite the stretch!

Alright folks, let's get to know your fabulous vagina a bit better! It's the ultimate multitasking tunnel in your body, complete with an elastic muscular structure and a soft flexible lining that's all about making things slide and feel sensational.

Now here's where it gets interesting: think of your vagina as the VIP entrance for the penis during those exciting moments of intimacy. But that's not all—it's also a pro at managing the monthly menstrual flow, directing it smoothly from the uterus. And during the grand finale, childbirth, your vagina transforms into a superstar birth canal, allowing the baby to make a dramatic entrance into the world.

So there you have it—the inside scoop on your amazing vagina anatomy! It's here to serve you in style, making sure life's adventures are both exciting and comfy!

CHAPTER 7

The Marvelous Uterus

Let's Start with the Basics

Welcome to the whimsical world of the uterus! This amazing organ, often called the "womb," plays a starring role in the intricate ballet of human reproduction. But not just that, this little jester has a lot more tricks up its sleeve.

Your uterus is a pear-shaped muscular organ located in your pelvis. It's not as boring as it sounds; it's like the superhero headquarters for baby-making. When you're not busy growing a human, the uterus is about the size of a clenched fist. But during pregnancy, it expands to accommodate the growing bundle of joy, reaching a capacity that would make Mary Poppins' magical bag proud.

Every month, the uterus gets all dressed up for

a party that nobody wants to attend—menstruation! It's like hosting a surprise bash and the guest of honor is always Aunt Flo. The uterus prepares a lavish endometrial lining, and when no baby shows up, it decides to redecorate by shedding it all. Talk about a monthly makeover!

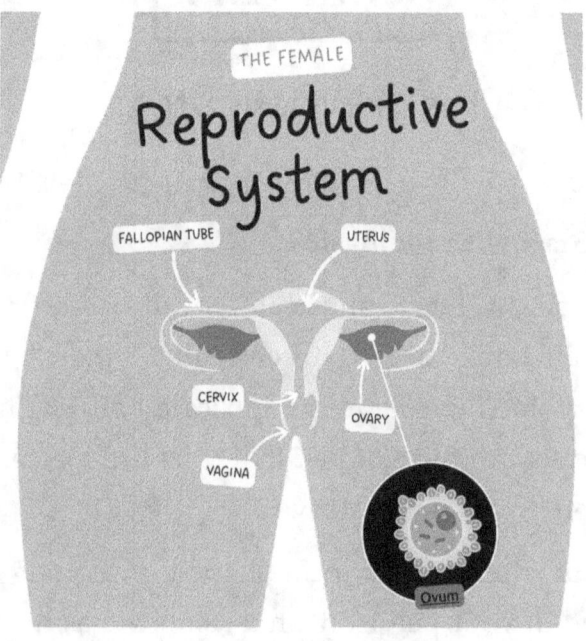

The female reproductive system includes parts of the female body that are involved in fertility, reproduction and sex. It includes organs such as the uterus, ovaries, fallopian tubes, cervix and vagina.

The Uterine Layers

Just like a good cake has layers, your uterus has three of them! There's the outermost layer, the perimetrium, which is like the frosting protecting the cake. Then comes the myometrium, the muscular middle layer responsible for those incredible contractions during labor. Finally, the innermost layer is the endometrium, which thickens and sheds during your menstrual cycle.

A Monthly Rollercoaster

Speaking of your menstrual cycle, your uterus plays a pivotal role. Each month, it prepares for the possibility of a baby. If no baby is on the way, it gracefully sheds its inner lining, resulting in menstruation. It's like the universe's way of saying, "NOT NOW!"

The Baby Bouncer

When pregnancy does occur, the uterus becomes the ultimate VIP lounge for your developing baby. It provides a safe and cozy space for nine months of growth, complete with room service (via the placenta) and a natural hot tub (amniotic fluid).

Uterus Factoids for the Curious

- Did you know that the uterus is one of the few organs that can expand exponentially and then shrink back to nearly its original size? It's like a real-life superhero cape.

- The uterus is incredibly strong. During childbirth,

it can exert a force equivalent to lifting a small car. Talk about girl power!

Some people even name their uteri. It's not uncommon to hear phrases like "My uterus, Lucy, is not happy today" in conversations among friends.

Uterus Fun Facts

- In ancient times, the uterus was thought to wander around the body, causing all sorts of problems. This theory, known as the "wandering womb," might seem a bit silly now, but it's a testament to the mysterious nature of this organ.

- A woman's uterus can weigh anywhere from 2 to 4 ounces, but during pregnancy, it can tip the scales at a whopping 2 pounds or more! That's like carrying around a mini watermelon.

Uterus: A Symbol of Strength

Your uterus is not just a biological marvel; it's a symbol of strength and resilience. It embodies the power to create and nurture life, making it one of the most remarkable organs in the human body. So whether you're a uterus owner or simply fascinated by the wonders of biology, take a moment to appreciate the beauty and complexity of this incredible organ. It truly deserves a standing ovation in the grand theater of life!

Hormone Hijinks

Our dear uterus isn't just a party planner; it's also a hormone hooligan. It produces prostaglandins, the tiny troublemakers that cause those delightful period cramps. It's like the neighborhood prankster ringing your doorbell and running away every month.

During pregnancy, the uterus becomes the hormone hoarder. It produces hCG, the hormone responsible for those telltale lines on pregnancy tests. It's like the uterus decided to corner the market on pregnancy signals.

Uninvited Houseguests

Occasionally, the uterus attracts some unwanted attention. Fibroids and polyps, those uninvited guests, show up for an extended stay. The main difference between fibroids and polyps is the tissue they are made of. They're like those distant relatives who never got the memo that the party's over. But don't worry; they can be shown the door if they overstay their welcome with the help of amazing healthcare providers.

The Overachieving PMS Poster Child

And let's not forget the uterus's flair for dramatic

entrances. It can throw quite the premenstrual party, complete with mood swings, cravings, and bloating. It's like auditioning for the role of the ultimate PMS poster child.

Unexpected Leaks and Mishaps

Just when you think things can't get more complicated, there are unexpected leaks and accidents. You might face situations in which your tampon might not stay in place or your pad might slip down your pant leg. It can be quite frustrating and inconvenient. But trust me, you are not the only one to whom it happened.

CHAPTER 8

Meet Olive, the Ovaries

Ovary Basics: Tiny but Strong

Welcome to the world of ovaries, those small but super important organs in your body. Think of them as egg keepers and hormone makers. They have a special job, and we're about to discover how they do it.

Ovaries may be small, but they are strong! Imagine them as egg holders. They keep your eggs safe until they are needed. But there's more to them than that.

Egg-citing Adventures

Ovaries have a fun task – they release eggs. It's like picking a special egg for a big adventure. This adventure is called making a baby, which takes two – an egg and a tiny swimmer called sperm.

The Hormone Helpers

Ovaries also make hormones. These are like messengers in your body. They tell your body what to do, like when to feel happy, hungry, or tired. Ovaries are like hormone factories making sure everything works smoothly.

Growing Up and Changing

Ovaries are your body's party starters during puberty. They begin the process of turning you from a kid into a teenager. You'll notice changes in your body and how you feel, all thanks to these little superheroes.

Surprises and How They Handle Them

Sometimes ovaries have surprises like cysts. These are like tiny bumps that can cause some discomfort. But ovaries are good at fixing things, and most of the time these surprises go away on their own.

Ovary Superstars

Ovaries work hard all your life, making sure everything is okay. They don't stop working until it's time for them to retire. So you can count on them to do their job well.

Fun Ovary Facts

- When you're born, you already have all the eggs you'll ever need in your ovaries. It's like having a secret stash of eggs ready for the future.

- Sometimes ovaries surprise you by releasing more than one egg. This can lead to twins or even more! It's like a surprise party with extra guests.

- Ovaries are great at doing many things at once. They handle eggs, make hormones, and deal with surprises like cysts. They're like the multitaskers of your body.

So, there you have it – ovaries, your body's egg protectors and hormone makers. They have a big job to do, and they're the heroes of your reproductive story.

CHAPTER 9

The Clitoris Chronicles: Discovering Your Joy Button

Hey there, friends! Get ready to uncover the secrets of something super cool: the clitoris! Think of it as your body's joy button, a tiny but powerful part that's all about feeling good and exploring your body's amazing abilities. Let's dive into the world of the clitoris and discover why it's so special.

A Clitoral History Lesson

The clitoris has had quite a journey through history. Ancient cultures saw it as a symbol of feminine power and pleasure. But over time, myths and misconceptions clouded its true purpose. Today, we know the clitoris deserves to be recognized as the center of pleasure.

Clitoris and Orgasms

The clitoris and orgasms go hand in hand. When stimulated, this magic button can create waves of pleasure, leading to orgasm. It's like the conductor of your body's symphony, orchestrating the ultimate crescendo of sensations.

Unique Shapes and Sizes

Every clitoris is unique! Just like snowflakes, no two are alike. Clitorises come in all shapes and sizes, just like people. Some like to stay hidden, while others are more out there, enjoying the spotlight. It's a reminder that we're all wonderfully different, and that's something to celebrate.

Beyond the Tip

While the clitoral tip is the part we often hear about, it's just the tip of the iceberg. Beneath the surface, the clitoris extends deep into the body like a hidden root system. It's like Mother Nature's secret garden, waiting to be explored.

The Clitoris in Action

The clitoris loves attention! It responds to different kinds of touch, from gentle caresses to more intense sensations. It's like having your very own pleasure dial, allowing you to explore what feels best for you.

Myths vs. Facts

- G-Spot Connection: Some people think the G-spot and the clitoris are the same, but they're like close friends, not twins. Learning about both can lead to exciting discoveries.

- Hidden Charms: Sometimes, the clitoris can be a little shy or hide beneath a protective hood. Getting to know your body and understanding these hidden charms can help you feel more comfortable and confident.

Celebrate Your Joy Button

In conclusion, the clitoris is like the rock star of your pleasure world. It's here to remind us that our bodies are designed for joy and exploration. So, embrace the clitoris, celebrate its incredible abilities, and remember that pleasure is a beautiful part of being human. Enjoy the adventure!

CHAPTER 10

All About Boobs:
Your Breast Friends

Welcome to the fantastic universe of breasts, those two buddies that ride along with you every day. In this chapter, we're going to explore the amazing world of boobs and get to know all about them.

Breasts: Nature's Masterpiece

Think of breasts as nature's masterpiece. They come in all shapes and sizes, and no two pairs are exactly alike. It's like Mother Nature's way of celebrating diversity.

More Than Just Eye Candy

Breasts aren't just there to look pretty; they have an important job. They can make milk to feed babies when you give birth, which is pretty amazing. It's like having a built-in milk factory!

The Hormone Connection

Your hormones are the conductors of the breast orchestra. They make your breasts swell, ache, or change throughout your menstrual cycle. It's like a monthly symphony directed by estrogen and progesterone.

The Support System

Your trusty bra is like a superhero sidekick, offering support and comfort. Wearing the right bra can make you feel great and keep your breast friends happy.

Check-Ups Are Important

Your breasts also teach you about taking care of your body. Checking them regularly can help find problems early, like breast cancer. Think of it as a self-care routine for your bosom buddies.

Myths and Facts

- Size Doesn't Matter: It doesn't matter if your breasts are big or small; you're amazing just as you are.

- No Perfect Match: Nobody has perfectly matching breasts. They're like snowflakes—each one is unique and that's perfectly normal.

- Nipple Nonsense: Nipples come in various shapes, sizes, and colors—each one is unique and wonderful.

Embrace Your Bosom Buddies

In conclusion, breasts are a fascinating and multi-dimensional part of your body. They're not just for looks; they play essential roles in nurturing, hormonal dance routines, and even self-confidence. So, embrace your bosom buddies, appreciate their uniqueness, and remember that they're a vital part of your incredible journey through life!

CHAPTER 11

Periods

The Grand Entrance

As you grow up, your body goes through lots of changes. One day, a special thing happens to your body, and that's when the Period makes its grand entrance.

Imagine your uterus collecting soft blankets and making it comfy. This is where a tiny baby could grow someday. To prepare for a possible baby visit, the uterus gets all cozy and warm.

No Baby? No Problem

If no baby decides to visit that month, your body says, "Well, we don't need this cozy nest right now." So, it cleans up the nest and starts fresh. That's the Period—a natural cleaning time for your body.

Mysterious Signals

Your body sends out special signals to tell you that the cleaning is happening. Sometimes, you might feel a little different during this time. Some people get mild tummy aches, mood swings, or feel tired. It's like a reminder that your body is doing its thing.

The Cycle Continues

This cleaning and getting ready process happens every month, like a never-ending story. It's a sign that your body is growing up, getting ready, and doing its amazing work.

So, don't worry when you hear about periods. It's just your body's way of keeping things neat and tidy inside. It's a natural part of growing up, and everyone's story is a little different. Embrace your unique tale, and remember, you're on an exciting adventure through the land of Growing Up!

The Journey into Womanhood

The journey into womanhood is an exciting adventure that comes with a monthly visitor—your period.

Onset of Menstruation

Your first period, or menarche, usually happens

between ages 9 and 16, with the average around 12. It's like a sign that your body is growing up and getting ready for amazing things.

Menstrual Cycle Phases

6. Menstrual Phase (Days 1-5): This is the start of your period, where your body says goodbye to the old lining of the uterus. It's like a gentle cleansing, and you might notice some blood and tissue.

7. Follicular Phase (Days 6-14): Imagine this as the preparation phase. Your body gears up for a potential baby. The ovaries get busy producing eggs, thanks to a hormone called FSH.

8. Ovulation (Around Day 14): This is the superstar moment! One of those eggs, all grown up in a sac called a follicle, is released from the ovary, ready to meet a special friend (sperm) for a possible baby-making dance.

9. Luteal Phase (Days 15-28): If the egg doesn't find its dance partner, your body takes a breather. Hormone levels shift, and the uterine lining starts to tidy up, making way for the next period.

Menstrual Hygiene

Taking care of yourself during your period is

crucial. Use pads or tampons to stay comfy and change them regularly. Also, make sure to dispose of used products properly to keep everything clean and healthy.

Emotional and Physical Changes

During your cycle, your emotions might be like a rollercoaster, and that's completely normal! You might feel moody, happy, or a bit of everything. Physical changes like mild cramps, bloating, and breast tenderness are common too.

Menstrual Education and Support

Learning about periods is super important. Parents, guardians, teachers, or health professionals can help you understand this natural process. Having open conversations and support makes the journey smoother and more comfortable.

Remember, everyone's experience is unique. If you ever have questions or concerns about your period, don't hesitate to talk to a healthcare professional. They're there to guide and support you on this incredible journey into womanhood!

Period Myths and Facts

Busting Period Myths

There are a lot of myths out there about periods. Let's set the record straight:

Myth: You can't swim during your period.

Fact: You absolutely can! Just use a tampon or menstrual cup.

Myth: Period blood is dirty.

Fact: Period blood is just blood and tissue from your uterus. It's not dirty at all.

Myth: You can't get pregnant during your period.

Fact: It's unlikely, but still possible. Always use protection if you're having sex.

Frequently Asked Questions

- How long should my period last?
- Most periods last 3-7 days.
- Is it normal to have irregular periods?
- Yes, especially when you first start. It can take a few years for your cycle to become regular.
- What if I have really bad cramps?
- Try using a heating pad, doing light exercise, or taking over-the-counter pain relievers if your

doctor recommends them.

Time-Traveling Through Periods: The Awesome Adventure of Lady in Red

While we may take our modern menstrual products and knowledge for granted, it's essential to understand how far we've come in our understanding of menstruation.

Let's explore the incredible journey of periods throughout the ages. Get ready for a rollercoaster ride of ancient mysteries, medieval myths, and 20th-century revolutions. Hold on to your hats and tampons, because it's going to be a wild ride!

Ancient Wonders

Picture this: Once upon a time, in ancient places like Egypt and Greece, people wondered about something strange—periods. They didn't understand why women bled each month. Some even thought women had magical powers. Talk about being mystical!

Medieval Mysteries

Now, let's jump to the Middle Ages. This was a time when people believed in weird things, like unicorns. Back then, they blamed women for bad things like crops dying because of their periods. Some even thought women were witches just because they had their period. Yikes!

Victorian Times

Imagine a time when people wore fancy clothes with tight corsets and petticoats. How did women handle their periods back then? Let's just say it involved lots of layers and some creative solutions. They sure had it tough, but they made it work.

1900s - Big Changes

Fast forward to the 1900s. This was when things got exciting. Disposable pads and tampons were invented, making life much easier for women during their periods. And in the 1900s, brave women started speaking up about periods. They said, "We're proud of our periods!"

Today's Cool Stuff

Now, let's come back to today. We have lots of cool stuff for periods, like menstrual cups and special underwear. Social media helps us talk about periods without feeling embarrassed. It's time to celebrate! We can talk openly about periods, have fun period parties, and enjoy some chocolate. Remember, having a period is natural and nothing to be ashamed of.

Cheers to the world of periods—it's a pretty amazing adventure!

Menstruation is no longer a secret – it's a story worth sharing!

Fun Period Facts

- Despite the fact that television and sanitary napkins are around the same age, it took until 1972 for the latter to be advertised on TV.

- Until as recently as 1972, advertisements for pads and tampons were prohibited on television. The ban persisted even after it was lifted, with ads resorting to the use of a misleading blue liquid instead of depicting actual blood to demonstrate absorbency.

- It wasn't until 1985, a staggering 13 years later, that the word "period" made its debut on TV in a Tampax commercial featuring a pre-Friends Courtney Cox.

- Two decades after Courtney Cox's ground-breaking ad, one would expect advertising to have progressed beyond reinforcing the idea that young girls should be discreet about their periods. Yet, in a 2005 Tampax commercial, the focus shifted to two students covertly passing a tampon in class. Instead of the girl openly acknowledging her menstrual cycle with pride, the discreet packaging becomes a tool for the girls to outsmart the teacher, allowing them to carry out their secret transaction without detection.

CHAPTER 12

The Fantastic Fiesta of Period Products

Hey, awesome reader! Welcome to the Period Product Party – where pads, tampons, cups, and period underwear are the VIP guests. Let's break down this fabulous feast of options and find out what suits your style!

Pad Paradise

Where comfort meets confidence. First up, we've got pads – the fluffy clouds that cradle you in comfort. They're the cushy armchair of the period world, coming in all shapes and sizes. From slim and discreet to the superhero overnighters, pads have your back (and your front!).

Tampon Town

The tiny trailblazers. Next on the list, we've got the Tampon Trio – Pearl, Ruby, and Sapphire. These little warriors are small but mighty, ready to take on the world with ease. They're like the queens of convenience, allowing you to keep doing your thing without missing a beat.

Cup Central

The reusable revolution continues. Now, let's dive into the world of menstrual cups – the eco-friendly champions. Imagine a tiny cupcake holder but for your flow. Once you get the hang of it, you'll be a cup-connoisseur, and the best part? It's reusable, making it a champion for both you and the planet.

Cloth Pad Corner

Where sustainability meets style (again). Picture a meadow of vibrant cloth pads, each one a mini work of art. These babies are like your favorite pair of undies but with a secret power to handle your flow. And guess what? You can wash and reuse them, making your period a little greener and a lot more stylish.

Underwear Utopia

Where comfort takes the spotlight. Now, let's

welcome the latest sensation – period underwear! These are like your favorite pair of comfy undies but with an extra layer of magic. They're designed to absorb and keep you feeling dry, making them perfect for lounging, exercising, or conquering the world – whatever floats your boat!

The world of period products includes tampons, pads, menstrual cups, period underwear, and reusable pads etc.

Now, here's the scoop – there's no one-size-fits-all solution. It's like picking your favorite flavor of ice cream – everyone has their preference. Some days you might feel like a pad princess and others a tampon tycoon.

Remember, it's all about what makes you feel fabulous. Mix and match, try different things, and embrace the variety of this fantastic fiesta. Because your period, my friend, is just a chapter in your incredible story, and with these options, you're ready to slay every page!

CHAPTER 13

The Awesome Tale of Peaches and Poop

Hey, cool kids! Let's talk about something super interesting – our bums and how they're called peaches!

Ever noticed people saying our bums look like peaches? Well, it's because peaches have two round halves, just like our bums! It's a fun way of saying our bums are pretty cool, just like peaches.

Our bums have lots of nicknames. From booty and buns to tushie and backside, people have all sorts of fun names for them. It's like having a bunch of nicknames for your best friend. So, when someone says 'gluteus maximus' (a big muscle in your buttock), they're just talking about our awesome bums!

No matter what you call it, it is important to know

the right name for it.

Poop Party: Where It All Happens

When we are talking about peaches, how can we forget to talk about poop? Let's talk about where our poop is stored—that place is called the rectum. It's a short tunnel that keeps our poop until our brain says it's time to go. Then, it's showtime out the back door!

Muscle Magic: Meet Your Bum Muscles

Our bums are more than just comfy seats. They have muscles – the gluteus maximus, medius, and minimus. These muscles help us do cool things like walking and running. So, next time you run or dance, thank your bum muscles!

Now, let's give a shoutout to our pelvic floor. It's a group of muscles that helps our poop move out smoothly. Teamwork, right?

Meet the levator ani muscle – the boss of our anus. It opens and closes the door when we need to go to the bathroom to get the poop out. Like a guardian protecting our exit!

The Cool Story of Poop

What's Healthy Poop?

So, what's healthy poop? Imagine soft-serve ice

cream – smooth, easy-going, not too hard or too squishy. Healthy poop is about finding that perfect balance – not too firm and definitely not too soft.

Colors of the Rainbow

Ever notice that poop comes in different colors? From browns to greens or even reds! It's like a magical rainbow. But here's the secret – the healthiest color is a nice shade of brown. Anything too different might be a sign to pay attention.

Why Healthy Poop Matters

Why does healthy poop matter? Well, think of it like this – your poop is a messenger. It tells a story about what's happening inside your body. Healthy poop means your digestive system is doing a great job!

The Plop, Plop, Plop

The sound your poop makes when it hits the water can also tell you something. A good 'plop, plop, plop' is like a victory song! It means your body is hydrated, and everything is moving just right. Celebrate those happy plops!

When Poop Gets Moody

But what if your poop is feeling a bit moody?

Maybe it's too hard, too soft, or just not cooperating. That's when you might want to think about what you're eating and drinking. Foods with fiber and staying hydrated are like superheroes for your digestive system.

How to Keep Poop Happy

Keeping poop happy is easy! Eat colorful fruits, veggies, and whole grains. Drink lots of water, and stay active. Your digestive system will be doing a happy dance, and so will your poop!

Let's Talk About It

Remember, talking about poop is totally okay! It's a natural part of being human, and understanding what's healthy helps you take care of your amazing body. So, embrace the rainbow, celebrate the plops, and keep your poop happy every day! ❄️ 💩

What's Constipation?

Imagine your tummy as a busy highway and constipation like a traffic jam. It happens when your poop decides to stick around for too long, making it hard and tricky to, well, make an exit.

Occasional straining to poop is not something to worry about. But regular straining while pooping can lead to health complications.

Why Constipation is Not Cool

So, why is constipation not cool? Picture your intestines like a highway, and poop as the cars trying to get through. When things slow down, poop gets stuck, and the longer it stays, the drier and harder it becomes. Not fun, right? We want our poop to move out easily.

The Impact on Your Pelvic Floor

Now, let's talk about your pelvic floor – the superhero team holding everything in place down there. When constipation hangs around, it puts extra pressure on this pelvic floor muscle. Your pelvic floor is like a trampoline – it needs to bounce back after doing its job. But when constipation stays, it's like having heavy stuff on the trampoline. Over time, it can affect your pelvic floor.

Straining Isn't a Superpower

Here's the deal – straining, or pushing hard to get poop out, is not a superpower. It can make things worse for your pelvic floor. Imagine your superheroes trying to hold up heavy stuff while you're pushing – not the best combo!

How to Beat Constipation

So, how do you beat constipation? Team up with fiber-rich foods, drink water like it's your superhero potion, and stay active. These are your allies in the fight against constipation. Also, no straining. Breathe as if you are blowing bubbles.

CHAPTER 14

Real Talk: What's Whack and When to Dial Up Your Doctor

Pelvic Pain Patrol

Alright, let's get real. It's normal to have some mild cramps during your period, but if you're experiencing intense or constant pain in your pelvic area, it's time to talk to your doctor or pelvic health physiotherapist. Pain while peeing or during bowel movements could also be signs that something's up down there.

Don't ignore persistent pelvic pain. This kind of discomfort could be a sign of some sneaky troublemakers like endometriosis, pelvic inflammatory disease (PID), ovarian cysts, or pelvic floor issues. These troublemakers can mess with your vibe and put a damper on your day. But don't sweat it—your healthcare provider should help you to find answers! They should help you and get to the bottom of what's causing all the commotion, Don't suffer in silence—reach out and get the help you need to kick those pelvic pain blues to the curb!

Period Pain Problems

Period cramps should not be a part of life and shouldn't stop you from doing your thing. If your cramps are so bad that they interfere with your daily activities, it's time to chat with your doctor or pelvic health physio. Keep an eye out for any changes in your period pain or if it suddenly gets worse over time. Your health care provider can help you figure out if your period pain is normal or if there's something else going on that needs to be addressed.

Discharge Drama

It's normal to have some vaginal discharge—it's your body's way of keeping things clean and healthy down there. But if you notice any changes in color, consistency, or smell of your discharge, it's worth bringing up with your doctor.

Discharge that's green, yellow, gray, frothy, or has a strong odor could be signs of an infection that needs treatment.

Itch and Burn Blues

Feeling itchy or burning down there isn't something you should just ignore. It could be a sign of a yeast infection, bacterial vaginosis, or another infection that needs to be treated. Don't suffer in silence—talk to your doctor if you're experiencing any discomfort or unusual sensations in your pelvic area.

Menstrual Cycle Madness

Your period might not always be like clockwork, but if you notice any significant changes in your menstrual cycle, it's worth mentioning to your health care provider. Things like suddenly missing periods, having irregular periods, or bleeding between periods could be signs that something's off. Your health care provider can help you figure out what's causing the changes and what steps you can take to get your cycle back on track.

Pain During Tampons/Intercourse/Periods/ Big Os

If using tampons or getting busy in the bedroom feels more like a pain-fest, it's time to talk to your doctor. Feeling discomfort during these activities could mean something up there, like an infection, endometriosis, or a wacky pelvic floor. But don't stress, your healthcare providers got your back!

They'll help figure out what's going on and how to fix it so you can get back to feeling fab. So don't suffer in silence—reach out and get the help you need!

Urinary or Bowel Changes

If you're running to the bathroom for a pee all the time, feeling pain when you pee, leaking when laugh or giggle, spotting blood in your urine, or noticing changes in your poop routine, it might mean something's off with your body. It could be stuff like UTIs, bladder problems, tummy issues, or pelvic floor issues. But don't sweat it! You can see a health care provider and figure out what's going on. So if you're feeling funky down there, don't be shy—let your healthcare provider know what's up so they can help you!

Concerns about Reproductive Health

If you're not sure about stuff like birth control, don't worry! Your health care providers know all about it and can help. Whether you're thinking about different ways to prevent pregnancy, they've got your back. Just ask them your questions, and they'll give you the info and support you need to make decisions about your body. So don't be afraid to talk to your doctor or trusted adult—they're there to help you with anything you need regarding your reproductive health! Consulting a healthcare provider can provide guidance and support.

When to Consult Health Care Pros

Though your vulva is remarkably self-sufficient, it's crucial to be aware of signs that indicate an imbalance or infection. If you notice any of the following, it's a good idea to consult a healthcare professional:

- Unusual Discharge: A change in the color, smell, or consistency of vaginal discharge.

- Itching or Irritation: Persistent itching, redness, or discomfort in the genital area.

- Burning Sensation: A burning sensation during urination could be a sign of infection.

- Unusual Odor: A strong, foul odor that is different from your normal scent.

- Pain with tampons and severe period pain.

- Painful Intercourse: Pain or discomfort during sexual intercourse.

Remember

Your pelvic health is important, and if anything feels off or not quite right, don't hesitate to reach out to your health care provider. They're there to help you stay healthy and feel your best, so don't be afraid to speak up and take care of yourself!

CHAPTER 15

Body Positivity and Self-Esteem

Loving Yourself: Embracing Body Positivity

Puberty brings a whirlwind of changes that can sometimes make you feel self-conscious. But remember, every change is a sign that your body is growing and developing just as it should. Embracing body positivity means loving yourself exactly as you are, changes and all. Here are some tips to boost your self-esteem:

- Focus on What Your Body Can Do: Instead of concentrating on how your body looks, think about all the amazing things it can do. Your legs help you run, your arms let you hug your friends, and your smile can light up a room.

- Surround Yourself with Positivity: Spend time with people who make you feel good about yourself. Avoid those who bring negativity into your life.

- Limit Social Media: Remember that social media often shows a highlight reel of someone's life. Don't compare your everyday moments to someone else's filtered and edited photos.

- Practice Self-Care: Take time for activities that make you feel happy and relaxed. Whether it's reading a book, taking a walk, or doing a fun hobby, self-care is vital for mental health.

Famous Quotes on Body Positivity

Here are some quotes from famous people who embrace body positivity:

- "You are more than your body, but that doesn't mean you should neglect it." - Demi Lovato

- "Confidence is the only outfit you can't buy. It's not for sale. You have to earn it." - Beyoncé

- "You are beautiful just the way you are." - Meghan Trainor

CHAPTER 16

Understanding Puberty and Hormonal Changes

What's Happening to My Body?

Puberty is a time of big changes, both inside and outside. Here's a rundown of what to expect:

- Hormonal Changes: Your body starts producing more hormones, which can affect your mood and cause physical changes like acne and growth spurts.

- Breast Development: Your breasts will start to grow, and it's totally normal for them to be sore sometimes.

- Hair Growth: You'll notice more hair under your arms, on your legs, and in your pubic area.

Dealing with Mood Swings

Hormonal changes can make your emotions feel like a rollercoaster. Here are some tips for dealing with mood swings:

- Talk It Out: Share your feelings with a friend, family member, or counselor.

- Stay Active: Exercise can help boost your mood and reduce stress.

- Eat Well: Eating a balanced diet can help keep your hormones in check.

CHAPTER 17

Healthy Lifestyle Choices

Healthy Habits for a Healthy Body

Hey, amazing squad! Let's chat about how to keep your bod in tip-top shape. Eating right, staying active, and catching those Zzzs are super crucial for your overall health, especially your pelvic health. Here's why these habits are totally lit:

Nutrition

Eating a balanced diet with lots of fruits, veggies, whole grains, and lean proteins fuels your body and keeps everything running smoothly. Foods high in fiber help prevent constipation, which is great for your pelvic health.

Exercise

Regular physical activity keeps your muscles

strong, including those in your pelvic area. Fun activities like walking, swimming, and yoga are fantastic options.

Sleep

Aim for 8-10 hours of sleep each night. Sleep is when your body recharges, so it's essential for staying healthy and energetic.

Good and Bad Bladder Habits

It's not the most glamorous topic, but taking care of your bladder is a super important part of a healthy life. Here are some good and bad habits that can make a big difference. Let's keep it real and fun!

Good Bladder Habits

- **Stay Hydrated:** Chug that H2O! Aim for about 6-8 glasses a day. Water keeps everything flowing smoothly and helps prevent those nasty infections.

- Answer Nature's Call: When you gotta go, you gotta go. Don't hold it in like a champ—your bladder needs relief.

- Wipe Right: After using the loo, always wipe front to back. Trust me, it helps keep the bad stuff away.

- Stay Fresh: Keep your downstairs clean and dry. Ditch sweaty clothes after sports and avoid super tight, synthetic undies.

- Eat Your Greens: Fiber-rich foods are your besties. They help you avoid constipation, putting less pressure on your bladder.

- Pee Post-Workout: Exercise can sometimes make you feel like you need to go. Listen to your body and hit the bathroom when you need to.

Bad Bladder Habits

- Skipping Water: If you're not guzzling enough water, your pee can become concentrated and irritate your bladder.

- Caffeine Overload: Sodas and energy drinks can be your bladder's enemy. They make you need to pee more often.

- Ignoring the Urge: Holding your pee for too long can mess with your bladder muscles and lead to infections. Not cool.

- Just in Case Trips: Peeing when you don't really need to can confuse your bladder, making it feel like you need to go more often than you really do.

- Tight Clothes: Rocking tight jeans and undies can

trap moisture and irritate your skin, saying hello to infections.

- Sugary Drinks: These drinks might taste great, but they can irritate your bladder and aren't great for your overall health.

Taking care of your bladder is all about balance. Drink water, listen to your body, and stay fresh. Your bladder will thank you!

Fun Tips for Staying Healthy

- Snack Smart: Keep yummy and healthy snacks like fruits, nuts, and yogurt handy for when you get hungry.
- Stay Hydrated: Drink plenty of water throughout the day. It helps your body function properly and keeps your skin glowing.
- Get Moving: Find an activity you love, like dancing, biking, or playing a sport, and make it a regular part of your routine.

Get Moving: Exercise and Your Pelvic Health

Staying active isn't just great for your overall health—it's also super beneficial for your pelvic health. Here's how:

- Strengthening Muscles: Exercises like squats, pushups, and long walks can strengthen your pelvic muscles.

- Reducing Stress: Physical activity releases endorphins, which help reduce stress and boost your mood.

- Improving Posture: Activities like yoga and Pilates improve your posture, which is fantastic for your pelvic health.

Fun Ways to Stay Active

- Dance Party: Turn up your favorite tunes and dance like nobody's watching. It's a fun way to get moving and feel great.

- Join a Team: Playing a sport with friends is a fun way to stay active and socialize. Whether it's soccer, basketball, or volleyball, team sports are awesome.

- Outdoor Adventures: Hiking, biking, and swimming are great ways to enjoy nature and get exercise. Plus, it's a chance to explore new places and have fun with friends.

Remember, taking care of your body is all about finding what you enjoy and making it a part of your everyday life. Stay active, eat well, and get plenty of sleep to keep your body and your pelvic health in prime condition!

CONCLUSION

Hooray you made it to the end of the book!
I am so happy you are here.

Welcome to the ideal world of my vision where every girl grows up with confidence and knowledge about her body, periods, and pelvic health—a world where discussions about such things are met with openness and understanding. In this world, there is no shame or embarrassment surrounding periods, and girls are empowered to embrace their bodies without fear of judgment or stigma.

Growing up in this world means living free from the confusion and uncertainty about what constitutes the "right" size or shape for a body. It means understanding and celebrating the diversity of bodies, knowing that beauty comes in all shapes, sizes, and forms.

In this world, there are no mysteries or taboos surrounding the vulva and vagina. Girls grow up with a clear understanding of their anatomy, empowered to advocate for their own health and well-being. They know that their bodies are miraculous and worthy of love, respect, and care.

It is my hope that this book serves as a guiding light to navigate the journey of adolescence, providing the knowledge and support needed to embrace pelvic health with confidence and pride. Together, let's create a world where every girl feels empowered, informed, and celebrated for who she is.

This book is a labor of love, born from a passion for empowering teens with essential knowledge about their bodies and pelvic health. As a pelvic health educator and physiotherapist, I've witnessed firsthand the transformative impact that understanding and prioritizing pelvic wellness can have on young lives. Repeat after me:

- I am enough. I do not have to change myself to be enough.

- I am always learning more about who I am and what matters to me.

- I accept and love the way I look without comparing myself to others.

- My body keeps me strong; my body keeps me healthy..

- I am beautiful and perfect the way I am; no one can tell me otherwise.

I am so proud of you for embracing this book, "Things Every Girl Should Know about Her Body." Throughout these pages, you found a wealth of information designed to demystify your body and equip you with the tools to navigate the journey of adolescence with confidence and resilience. From understanding your menstrual cycle to embracing body positivity, from practicing self-care to fostering healthy relationships—every topic is approached with care, compassion, and inclusivity.

I want to emphasize that your pelvic health is not just about physical well-being; it's about empowerment, self-awareness, and self-love. By embracing the knowledge shared in this book, you're taking a powerful step towards advocating for your own health and mental wellness.

I encourage you to approach this journey with an open mind and a sense of curiosity. Your body is incredible, and understanding it is a journey worth embarking on. Remember, you are not alone on this path. I am here to support you every step of the way.

Thank you for entrusting me with your health education. My hope is that this book illuminates the path towards a lifetime of pelvic wellness and empowerment.

xo Richa

MEET RICHA PALIYA-REHAN

Meet Richa Paliya- Rehan – Owner of Harmony Physiotherapy and Athletico Sports physiotherapy in eastern Ontario, Richa is a successful entrepreneur, women's health educator, and physiotherapist extraordinaire!

With a global mission to amplify the importance of prioritizing our health, especially when it comes to women's health, Richa is leading the charge in breaking barriers and sparking conversations.

As a fierce advocate for women's well-being, Richa is dedicated to empowering South Asian Women to take control of their health journey, fearlessly discussing topics ranging from physical fitness to sexual health.

Richa's mission is crystal clear: to equip women with the knowledge and tools they need for a fulfilling pelvic health journey – from periods and pregnancy to postpartum and menopause.

Fuelled by a passion for making a difference, Richa is committed to transforming lives, one pelvis at a time. And when she's not immersed in the intricacies of pelvic anatomy, she's embracing the joyous chaos of motherhood with her spirited almost-5-year-old mini-me.

- Instagram: @thepelvicexperts
- Contact: learnwith.richarehan@gmail.com

THANK YOU FOR READING MY BOOK

Dear Reader,

Thank you from the bottom of my heart for embarking on this journey with me. Writing this book has been a labor of love, and I am deeply grateful for the opportunity to share my knowledge and passion for pelvic health with you.

To every teen, parent, educator, healthcare professional, and advocate who picks up this book, I extend my sincerest gratitude. Your interest and dedication to promoting pelvic health awareness among teens is truly inspiring.

Thanks to the teens who are navigating their pelvic health journey: you are brave, resilient, and worthy of all the support and resources available to you.

Remember, you are not alone, and your health and well-being matter.

As you close this book, I hope you feel informed, empowered, and inspired to prioritize your pelvic health and advocate for others.

Together, we can create a world where pelvic health, period health, and women's health is recognized, respected, and supported for all.

With heartfelt thanks, I really appreciate all of your feedback and I love hearing what you have to say. I need your input to make the next version of this book and my future books better. Please take two minutes now and leave a helpful review on Amazon letting me know what you thought of the book.

Thanks so much!

Richa Paliya-Rehan

MY GIFT TO YOU

I am so glad you're here!

As my Gift to you, get FREE Access to the
Audiobook of
Things Every Girl Should Know About Her Body
and other Free Resources by scanning the QR Code
below or visiting
www.RichaRehan.com

www.ingramcontent.com/pod-product-compliance
Lightning Source LLC
Chambersburg PA
CBHW071202120626
46546CB00006B/2383